GOD OF OUR FATHERS

THREE PATRIOTIC HYMNS OF FAITH

ARRANGED BY

Carolyn Hamlin

Table of Contents

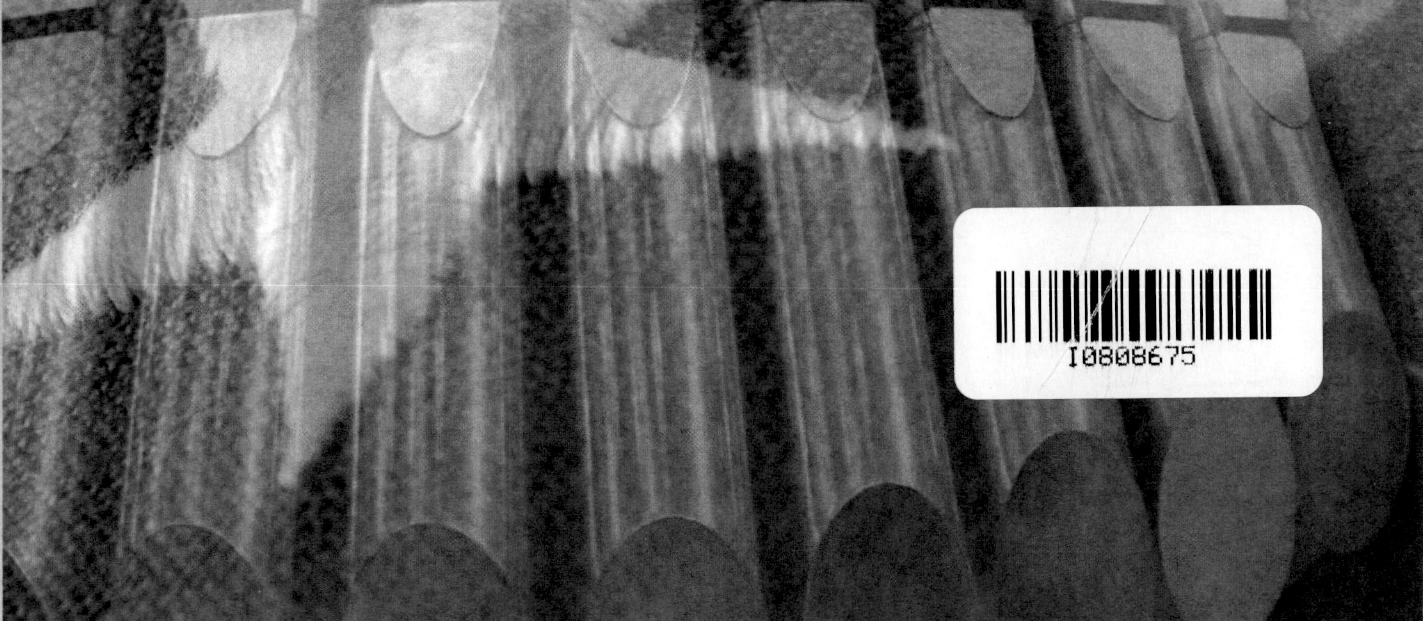

for Jim and Sarah Ingram

Eternal Father, Strong to Save

REGISTRATIONS:
Due to the complexity of the suggested registrations (both traditional and MIDI), they are included separately on pages 11-12.

MELITA
John B. Dykes
Arr. by Carolyn Hamlin

With prayerful fervor (♩ = 88)

9
13
Gen. 2
Sw.
Gt.
17
21
Sw. 1
Ch.
Gt.

25
29
Gen. 3
Gt.
Ch.
Gt.
33
37
Gen. 4

41
Gen. 5
Gt.
Ch.
Ch.
45
48
51

54
Gen. 4
Gt.
rit.
Gen. 6
Ch.
Gt.
58
With feeling
61
Gt.
64

Gen. 7
Ch.
Gt.
rit.
Gen. 8
Gt.
Much broader

80
Ch.
83
85
Gt.
89
Gen. 9
3

93
Full Organ, no Reeds
96
99
Full Organ, with Reeds
gradual rit.
102
Ped. 1

TRADITIONAL REGISTRATION

GENERAL 1: Sw. Trumpet 8'
Gt. Diapason 8' (or Principal), Harmonic Flute 8', Octave 4', Spitzflute 4', Ch. to Gt. 8'
Ch. Gedeckt 8', Principal 4', Koppelflute 4'
Ped. Bourdon 32', Bourdon 16', Violone 16', Gt. to Ped. 8', Ch. to Ped. 8'

GENERAL 2: Sw. Waldhorn 16', Piccolo 2', Trem.
Gt. Harmonic Flute 8', Gamba 8'
Ch. Krummhorn 8' (or Clarinet 8')
Ped. Violone 16', Gt. to Ped. 8'
Sw. Divisional: Trumpet 8'

GENERAL 3: Sw. Viola 8', Viola Celeste 8', Vox Humana 8', Trem.
Gt. Gamba 8', Trem., Sw. to Gt. 8', Ch. to Gt. 8'
Ch. Viole 8', Viole Celeste 8', Trem.
Ped. Violone 16', Lieblich Bourdon 16', Sw. to Ped. 8', Ch. to Ped. 8'

GENERAL 4: Sw. Bourdon 8', Viola 8', Principal 4'
Gt. Diapason 8', Harmonic Flute 8', Octave 4', Sw. to Gt. 16', Sw. to Gt. 8'
Ch. Festival Trumpet 8'
Ped. Bourdon 32', Bourdon 16', Violone 16', Flute 8', Gt. to Ped. 8', Sw. to Ped. 8'

GENERAL 5: Sw. Bourdon 8', Nazard 2⅔'
Gt. Spitzflute 4', Sw. to Gt. 4'
Ped. Violone 16', Flute 8'

GENERAL 6: Sw. Viola 8', Viola Celeste 8', Bourdon 8', Flute Celeste II 8', Flute 4', Trem., Sw. to Gt. 8', Sw. to Gt. 4', Ch. to Gt. 8'
Gt. Diapason 8', Gamba 8', Octave 4', Flute 4', Trem., Sw. to Gt. 8, Sw. to Gt. 4', Ch. to Gt. 8'
Ch. Viole 8', Viole Celeste 8', Gedeckt 8', Koppelflute 4', Trem.
Ped. Violone 32', Bourdon 16', Violone 16', Sw. to Ped. 8', Ch. to Ped. 8'

GENERAL 7: Sw. Viola 8', Principal 4', Mix. IV, Waldhorn 16' (or Bassoon), Trumpet 8', Clarion 4'
Gt. Diapason 8', Octave 4', Sw. to Gt. 8'
Ch. Festival Trumpet 8'
Ped. Bourdon 32', Diapason 16', Bourdon 16', Violone 16', Octave 8', Gt. to Ped. 8', Sw. to Ped. 8'

GENERAL 8: Sw. Viola 8', Principal 4', Mix. IV, Waldhorn 16' (or Bassoon), Trumpet 8', Clarion 4'
Gt. Violone 16', Diapason 8', Octave 4', Twelfth 2⅔', Fifteenth 2', Sw. to Gt. 8'
Ch. Festival Trumpet 8'
Ped. Bourdon 32', Diapason 16', Bourdon 16', Violone 16', Octave 8', Bombarde 16', Gt. to Ped. 8'

GENERAL 9: Sw. Viola 8', Principal 4', Mix. IV, Waldhorn 16' (or Bassoon), Trumpet 8', Clarion 4'
Gt. Violone 16', Diapason 8', Octave 4', Twelfth 2⅔', Fifteenth 2', Sw. to Gt. 8'
Ch. Festival Trumpet 8'
Ch. MIDI: Bugle + MIDI on Ch.
Ped. Bourdon 32', Diapason 16', Bourdon 16', Violone 16', Octave 8', Bombarde 16', Gt. to Ped. 8'
Gen. Ch. to Gt. Melody Coupler

GENERAL 10: Sw. Viola 8', Principal 4', Mix. IV, Waldhorn 16' (or Bassoon), Trumpet 8', Clarion 4'
Gt. Violone 16', Diapason 8', Octave 4', Twelfth 2⅔', Fifteenth 2', Double Trumpet 16', Tromba 8', Sw. to Gt. 8', Sw. to Gt. 4', Ch. to Gt. 8'
Ch. Gedeckt 8', Principal 4', Octave 2', Quinflute 1⅓', Scharf III
Ped. Bourdon 32', Diapason 16', Bourdon 16', Violone 16', Octave 8', Choral Bass 4', Bombarde 16' Trompette 8', Gt. to Ped. 8', Sw. to Ped. 8', Ch. to Ped. 8'
Ped. Divisional I: Bourdon 32', Diapason 16', Bourdon 16', Violone 16', Octave 8', Choral Bass 4' Bombarde 16', Trompette 8', Gt. to Ped. 8', Sw. to Ped. 8', Ch. to Ped. 8'

MIDI REGISTRATION

(* = tremolo)

GENERAL 1:
Sw. MIDI: Bugle* + MIDI on Sw.
Gt. Diapason 8' (or Principal), Harmonic Flute 8', Ch. to Gt. 8'
Gt. MIDI: Solo Violin* + MIDI on Gt.
Ch. Viole 8', Viole Celeste 8'
Ped. Bourdon 32', Bourdon 16', Violone 16', Gt. to Ped. 8', Ch. to Ped. 8'
Ped. Divisional I: Ped. Bourdon 32', Bourdon 16', Violone 16', Gt. to Ped. 8', Ch. to Ped. 8'
Ped. MIDI: Tympani + MIDI on Ped.

GENERAL 2:
Sw. MIDI: Bassoon
Gt. Harmonic Flute 8'
Ch. MIDI: Clarinet + MIDI on Ch.
Ped. Violone 16', Gt. to Ped. 8'
Sw. Divisional I: Sw: MIDI Muted Trumpet + MIDI on Sw.

GENERAL 3:
Sw. Viola 8', Viola Celeste 8', Vox Humana 8', Trem.
Gt. Gamba 8', Trem., Sw. to Gt. 8', Ch. to Gt. 8'
Gt. MIDI: Solo Violin* + MIDI on Gt.
Ch. Gamba 8', Trem., Sw. to Gt. 8', Ch. to Gt. 8'
Ped. Violone 16', Lieblich Bourdon 16', Sw. to Ped. 8', Ch. to Ped. 8'
Ped. MIDI: Violone 16', Lieblich Bourdon 16', Sw. to Ped. 8', Ch. to Ped. 8'
Ped. MIDI: Solo Violin* + MIDI on Ped.

GENERAL 4:
Sw. Bourdon 8', Viola 8', Principal 4'
Sw. MIDI: Brass Ensemble + MIDI on Sw.
Gt. Diapason 8', Harmonic Flute 8', Octave 4', Sw. to Gt. 16', Sw. to Gt. 8'
Gt. MIDI: Brass Ensemble + MIDI on Gt.
Ch. Festival Trumpet 8'
Ch. MIDI: Bugle + MIDI on Ch.
Ped. Bourdon 32', Bourdon 16', Violone 16', Flute 8', Gt. to Ped. 8', Sw. to Ped. 8'
Ped. MIDI: Brass Ensemble + MIDI on Ped.

GENERAL 5:
Sw. MIDI: Piccolo + MIDI on Sw.
Gt. MIDI: Clarinet + MIDI on Ch.
Ped. MIDI: Bassoon + MIDI on Ped.

GENERAL 6:
Sw. Viola 8', Viola Celeste 8', Bourdon 8', Flute Celeste II 8', Flute 4', Vox Humana 8', Trem.
Gt. Diapason 8', Gamba 8', Octave 4', Flute 4', Trem., Sw. to Gt. 8', Sw. to Gt. 4', Ch. to Gt. 8'
Gt. MIDI: Solo Violin* + MIDI on Gt.
Ch. Viole 8', Viole Celeste 8', Gedeckt 8', Koppelflute 4', Trem.
Ch. MIDI: Solo Violin* + MIDI on Ch.
Ped. Violone 32', Bourdon 16', Violone 16', Sw. to Ped. 8', Ch. to Ped. 8'
Ped. MIDI: Cello B* + MIDI on Ped.

GENERAL 7:
Sw. Viola 8', Principal 4', Mix. IV, Waldhorn 16' (or Bassoon), Trumpet 8', Clarion 4'
Gt. Diapason 8', Octave 4', Sw. to Gt. 8'
Ch. Festival Trumpet 8'
Ch. MIDI: Bugle + MIDI on Ch.
Ped. Bourdon 32', Diapason 16', Bourdon 16', Violone 16', Octave 8', Gt. to Ped. 8', Sw. to Ped. 8'

GENERAL 8:
Sw. Viola 8', Principal 4', Mix. IV, Waldhorn 16' (or Bassoon), Trumpet 8', Clarion 4'
Gt. Violone 16', Diapason 8', Octave 4', Twelfth 2⅔', Fifteenth 2', Sw. to Gt. 8'
Ch. Festival Trumpet 8'
Ch. MIDI: Bugle + MIDI on Ch.
Ped. Bourdon 32', Diapason 16', Bourdon 16', Violone 16', Octave 8', Bombarde 16', Gt. to Ped. 8' Sw. to Ped. 8'

GENERAL 9:
Sw. Viola 8', Principal 4', Mix. IV, Waldhorn 16' (or Bassoon), Trumpet 8', Clarion 4'
Gt. Violone 16', Diapason 8', Octave 4', Twelfth 2⅔', Fifteenth 2', Mix. IV, Sw. to Gt. 8'
Ch. Festival Trumpet 8'
Ch. MIDI: Bugle + MIDI on Ch.
Ped. Bourdon 32', Diapason 16', Bourdon 16', Violone 16', Octave 8', Bombarde 16', Gt. to Ped. 8' Sw. to Ped. 8'

GENERAL 10:
Sw. Viola 8', Principal 4', Mix. IV, Waldhorn 16' (or Bassoon), Trumpet 8', Clarion 4'
Gt. Violone 16', Diapason 8', Octave 4', Twelfth 2⅔', Fifteenth 2', Double Trumpet 16', Tromba 8', Sw. to Gt. 8', Sw. to Gt. 4', Ch. to Gt. 8'
Ch. Gedeckt 8', Principal 4', Octave 4', Quinflute 1⅓', Scharf III
Ped. Bourdon 32', Diapason 16', Bourdon 16', Violone 16', Octave 8', Choral Bass 4', Bombarde 16' Trompette 8', Gt. to Ped. 8', Sw. to Ped. 8', Ch. to Ped. 8'
Ped. Divisional I: Bourdon 32', Diapason 16', Bourdon 16', Violone 16', Octave 8', Choral Bass 4' Bombarde 32', Bombarde 16', Trompette 8', Gt. to Ped. 8', Sw. to Ped. 8', Ch. to Ped. 8'
Ped. MIDI: Tympani + MIDI on Ped.

for my dear friend, Joan Kotrady

God of Our Fathers

Sw. Trumpet 8', Octave 4'
Gt. Diapason 8', Harmonic Flute 8', Octave 4', Fifteenth 2', Mix. IV, Ch. to Gt. 8'
Ch. Gedeckt 8', Principal 4', Octave 2', Quintflote 1⅓'
Ped. Bourdon 16', Gedeckt 8', Ch. to Ped. 8'

NATIONAL HYMN
George W. Warren
Arranged by Carolyn Hamlin

Pomposo, maestoso (♩ = 92)

9
a tempo
12
Sw.
slight rit.
15
a tempo
18

21
24
27
30
slight rit.
Gt.

Sw. Viola 8', Bourdon 8', Principal 4'
Gt. Diapason 8', Harmonic Flute 8', Sw. to Gt. 8', Ch. to Gt. 8'
Ch. Gedeckt 8', Flute 4'
Ped. Bourdon 16', Violone 16', Sw. to Ped. 8'

46
49
Add: Sw. Piccolo 2', Mix. IV
Gt. Mix. IV
Ch. Octave 2'
Ped. Octave 8', Gt. to Ped. 8', Ch. to Ped. 8'
52
(♮)
55

Add: Sw. Trumpet 8', Waldhorn 16'
Gt. Twelfth 2⅔', Tromba 8'
Ch. Octave 2', Scharf IV
Ped. Diapason 16', Trompette 8'

70
Full organ, with reeds
73
much broader
76
79
molto rit.
Ped. +Bombarde 32'

for Dr. Sidney L. Buckley

My Country, 'Tis of Thee

(God Save the Queen)

Sw. Trumpet 8'
Gt. Diapason 8', Harmonic Flute 8', Octave 4', Spitzflute 4'
Ch. Gedeckt 8', Principal 4', Koppelflute 4', Ch. to Gt. 8'
Ped. Bourdon 16', Violone 16', Gt. to Ped. 8', Ch. to Ped. 8'

Tune: NATIONAL ANTHEM
From *Thesaurus Musicus*, 1744
Arr. by Carolyn Hamlin

With patriotic fervor ♩ = 90

12
Sw.
16
Gt.
20
Sw.
24

Ch.
Sw. Viola 8', Viola Celeste 8', Vox Humana 8', Trem.
Gt. Gamba 8', Trem., Sw. to Gt. 8', Ch. to Gt. 8'
Ch. Viole 8', Viole Celeste 8', Sw. to Ch. 8'
Ped. Violone 16', Lieb. Bourdon 16', Sw. to Ped. 8', Gt. to Ped. 8'
rit.
Ch.
a tempo
Gt.

Sw. Bourdon 8', Principal 4', Mixture IV
Gt. Diapason 8', Harmonic Flute 8'. Octave 4', Sw. to Gt. 8', Ch. to Gt. 8'
Ch. Gedeckt 8', Principal 4', Octave 2', Quintflute 1⅓'
Ped. Bourdon 16', Violone 16', Octave 8', Gt. to Ped. 8', Sw. to Ped. 8', Ch. to Ped. 8'

Sw. Viola 8', Principal 4', Mix. IV, Waldhorn 16', Trumpet 8', Clarion 4'
Gt. Diapason 8', Octave 4', Super Octave 2', Sw. to Gt. 8'
Ch. Festival Trumpet
Ped. Diapason 16', Bourdon 16', Violone 16', Octave 8', Bombarde 16', Gt. to Ped. 8', Gt. to Ped. 8'